COXHOE & KELLOE *revisited 2*

COXHOE & KELLOE
REVISITED
2

'Coxhoe & Kelloe *revisited 2*'
First Published in England in the United Kingdom
in the year 2011
'Bermac Publications Newton Aycliffe
www.bermac.co.uk
E-Mail bmccormick@bermac.co.uk

© Bernard McCormick 2011

All rights reserved. No part of this publication
May be reproduced or stored in a retrieval system.
Nor transmitted in any form, electronic or mechanical. It can
not be recorded or photocopied or used in any other way
without prior permission of the Publisher or copyright holder.

ISBN 978-0-9568167-7-1

Typesetting and originating by
Bermac Publications.
Printed and Bound in Great Britain by
Newton Press, Newton Aycliffe.

FOREWORD

In only three weeks after completing my last book 'Coxhoe & Kelloe *revisited*', I had received enough material to complete a further book in this series. It would be shameful if future generations never saw these wonderful photographs from their families now in the past; so I decided to produce a further book on the area. 'Coxhoe & Kelloe *revisited* 2', as always, I have tried to capture family life as it went on.

Terry Hadfield contacted me with an amazing set of photograph's mainly from school days at Kelloe, they are absolute gems. I feel sure that people from Coxhoe and Kelloe will appreciate the chance to see friends from the area, now probably in their seventies; Terry's collection features people the likes of Garbutt Richardson, Garbutt was a brilliant footballer, signing professional forms, but he died very young. Others featured are George Norman, Billy Powell, Jack Woodward, Brian Luke, Colin Weir, Terry McDonnell, Alfie Webb, R. Hesler, G. Robson, Jimmy Strong & M. Stoves to name just a few. Part of his collection was members of Coxhoe Workingmen's Club from many years ago. Jimmy Ord, Pincer Wilson, Jad Carr, Mr. Weirs, George Hadwin & Norman Robson, again just to mention a few. Terry's grandparents on their Diamond wedding, Mary and Isaac Hadfield, how many people in the present day will stay together sixty years; Mary Hadfield came to my home regularly and talked with my mother for hours about days in the past before discussing baking, cooking. I was always amazed at two people really enjoying conversation.

Denise Heward sent me some photographs of her family and on the male side their involvement in the British army in the first world war Anthony Stokes Denise's G Grandfather served with the 'Kings Own Lancashire' regiment on the Eastern front at Salonika later back at Coxhoe, Anthony was on the initial Committee that formed Coxhoe Co-op Store, Denise also sent me a photograph of a Coxhoe girls club photographed around 1959; this would seem a well organised club and I recognise many Coxhoe family names.

Margaret Heslington, the Granddaughter of James Laing, sent me some brilliant photograph's of the Laing & Oliver families; the early family shows they were a very powerful Coxhoe family having at least three successful Inn's around the 1900's also taking possession of 'Grange Farm' about 1895, the Charabanc days out shows a tremendous public support. Later the photograph's show the family progress from James Laing's involvement with the British Expeditionary Force in France where he served with three different Regiments. James stayed with the British forces until the very finish of hostilities, even though he suffered with the affects of being gassed. Later the family survived intact after the 1926 recession. The Laing family are a very humble and unpretentious family that built their business over the years by sheer hard work and it has been a pleasure featuring them in the book.

For many years the TMS bus service served Coxhoe, Kelloe and in fact the whole of South West Durham; the bus service was such a success that Philip Kirk and Peter Cardno wrote and compiled a brilliant book about the Company. Philip gave me exclusive rights to reproduce parts of the story and graphics.

Above: Isaac Hadfield, Billy Wilson, G. Hadfield, Maureen Hadfield.

Below: G. Hadfield, Mr. Weirs, all on Coxhoe Club Trip.

DIAMOND WEDDING Isaac & Mary Hadfield of Coxhoe, both look very proud of the occasion and so they should be.

Above, L/R: George Hadfield, Jimmy Ord, Jad Carr, I Hadfield, Pincer Wilson.

CLUB TRIP:

Left: George Hadfield, with Jimmy Wilson.

The Hadfield's having a day out at Durham Big Meeting in the fifties, Uncle Gordon, Mam Mrs Hadfield, Aunt Evelyn, Terry Hadfield with his wife Audrey and Dad George Hadfield.

Above: Miners Gala, having a drink at the Sun Inn, Durham, Mr and Mrs Hadfield, John Malloy, Bish Mole and Wife.

Left: Miners Gala, July 1950.

Below: Uncle Jim with a young Terry Hadfield at 129 The Grove.

Above, L/R: Mrs. Hadfield, Mary Tickell, George Hadwin, George Hadfield, ?, Norman Robson.

Below: 'Coxhoe Carnival', 1950, taken by Terry Hadfield at Park Hill, Jimmy Hadfield (King), Deb Thompson (Jester), George Hadfield (Queen).

Above: 'Coxhoe Club', L/R: Granddad Isaac Hadfield, Mam Meggie, Dad George.
Below left: Harry Wilson, Grandma's brother. Below right, L/R: Dad George, Uncle Gordon, Grandma Mary Hadfield.

Page 12: A brilliantly clear photograph of Coxhoe Club members group, about 1940/50.
Photo from Terry Hadfield's Collection

Known group members: D. Thompson, Jack Scott, Mr. Mayo, Mr. Crook, Mickey Deacas junior & senior, Billy Platts, Mr. Hadwin, George Hadfield, Mr. Simmons, Wilson brothers, Eric Simmons, Mr. Barron, Isaac Hadfield.

Norman Dowding; probably taken near Burnett Crescent, Kelloe.

The 'Victoria', later traded as 'The Cricketers', was the sport pub of the area for years 'Coxhoe Athletic' used to change here and walk to the field next to the Cricket Club; I supported the team when very young when 'Stan Malcolm' was my idol, Uncle Al Ord was landlord at that time. Below: 'The Red Lion, a well known pub in Coxhoe Main Street, previously known as the 'Widows'. This was mainly my local and where there was a series of Landlords; one being my friend Jack Jones. The characters that used the pub were amazing people; just one of these Lukey Hammond and his son was reputed or alleged to have every set of Dominoes marked. Both father and son were first rate card sharp's and could deal any opposing player a pile of aces and himself a pile of three's in 'three card brag'. There was also character dart's players who could record a score on the board faster than a mathematician and were thought dunces at school but quickened their minds scoring pub games.

LEAGUE WINNERS Kelloe School Team 1953

R. Ruddock (teacher), J. Woodward, R. Johnson, T. Hadfield,
J. Strong, D. Beamson, R. Ward, B. Gregory, W. Powell, S. Marr,
G. Richardson, J. Huitson, B. Wear, right, (headmaster) Mr. Thompson.

Below:
KELLOE SCHOOLS LEAGUE (ENGLISH SCHOOLS LEAGUE),
played at Kingsway Bishop Auckland beat Bishop Auckland boys 4-3.
L/R: R. Ayre, T. Hadfield, B. Salmon, Purvis, J. Strong,
B. Walker, R. Middleton, D. Young, J. Lowes, G. Richardson, ?.
Later played Sunderland Boys 8000 crowd at Roker Park beat 2-0.

Steetley SC, lost 7-1 to Hordon, C.W. Durham County Challenge Cup. L/R: G. Rees, T. Hatfield, S. Marr, R. Hutton, V. Varvill, B. Armstrong, A. Armstrong, H. Stephenson, K. Ward, B. Harker, B. Weir.
Below: Some faces in the crowd, Alfie Salisbury, Ronnie Smith, Ray Barber, Gordon Willey.

B&O SHIELD WINNERS

B&O SHIELD NAMES

Page 17: Back Row, L/R: Derek Beamson, Keith Gaskill, Jim Strong, Ted Handley, Keith Peters, Charlie Austen, Ray Hesler, Terry Hadfield.

2nd Row: Colin Woodward, Billy Raine, Colin Kane, Keith Johnson, George Ward, Maurice Crathorne, George Strong, Jack Handley, Ted Dakin, Alfie Webb.

3rd Row: Bobby Morris, Garbutt Richardson, Kenny Fisher, Colin Weir, Cliff Seaton.

Front Row: Matty Davison, Billy Mitchell, Bob Davies, Reuben Dowding, Tom Woodward, Billy Dixon, Ray Tate, Brian Steel.

The school at this time featured 31 players on this photograph that maybe took part in this competition and it shows Kelloe school being proud of their success and connection to football; some names to note being Rueben Dowding was shown as Captain holding the large and magnificent shield, Billy Raine, second left middle, George Strong, or could be Billy Strong, seemed taller than the rest, 4th from right (middle), George was a brilliant footballer and so was his brother Jimmy, how they were not professional is a mystery, Colin Wear (Corky), second right 3rd row, now a very good show leek grower.

Jimmy Strong

Brian Luke

St. Williams R.C. School Team, Trimdon.
Back Row, L/R: Chesney Brighouse, Walton, Tommy Moore, John Hogg, Dennis Cooper, John Tinkler.
Front Row, L/R: Terry McDonald, Gerry Brown, Ken Chaytor, Joe (Yacker) Harrison, John Darby.
Below: Trimdon Village, the school was situated about two miles from the Village.

Vance Hudson's 40th Wedding Anniversary held at Peterlee Catholic Club, 31st Jan 02.
L/R: Terry Hadfield, Vance Hudson, Billy Powell.

Below: Skegness 1956, Vance Hudson and Terry Hadfield travelling by train to Lincoln then to Skegness.

Above: First holiday after leaving school at Blackpool 1955; everyone bought blue jeans.
L/R: George Norman, Billy Powell, Jack Woodward, Brian Luke, Terry Hadfield, unknown girls.

Below: Skegness 1957. L/R: Alan Hopper, Colin Weir, Terry McDonnell, Brian Luke, Billy Powell, Alfie Webb, Sammy Holden, Terry Hadfield.

Above: Dinner time Butlins, Filey 1958. L/R: G. Norman, B. Smith, T. Hadfield, C. Thompson, B. Powell, B. Weir.

Below: Filey, 'Sportsman Bar'. L/R: B. Powell. B. Smith, T. Hadfield, C. Thompson.

Skegness 1959. L/R: T. Hadfield, G. Norman, B. Powell, G. Robson, Matt Stoves, T. McDonnell, E. Caruthers, R. Hesler.

Below: Terry Hadfield playing the washboard with a group in a talent contest which made the London Newspapers (*4 London lads and a Durham miner*) won £25.

Left: Garbutt Richardson played football for Huddersfield & Everton. Garbutt died very young.

Above right: Kelloe Lads at Skegness 1954.
Below left: A similar earlier photograph & bottom right: Skegness 1959.
L/R: B. Powell, C. Weir, B. Luke, A. Webb, M. Stoves, G. Robson, T. McDonnell, G. Norman, T. Hadfield, R. Hesler, as above right, on the beach at FILEY.

Mr. & Mrs. Ward with their two sons at Kelloe. Date unknown, but again photographed by J. W. Chambers of West Cornforth; there appeared to be many Photographers in the area obviously all making a living.

From time to time you get some very interesting information from some families; the following mail was sent by Bill Marshall; 'My wife's maiden name was Bayles, her mothers maiden name was Ward, her father being in the photo on page 242 *(above) on the right named Robert Septimus as he was reputed to be the seventh son of a seventh son. Her grandmother was a Ramshaw sister to Jack, Ida, May, Billy and Gladys. Ida married a Lockey and Lockeys buildings was named after them in Coxhoe. Merry Christmas Bill.

In the photo on page 137 in the book '**Coxhoe & Kelloe revisited**' girl 6th from right middle row is Muriel Ramshaw sister-in-law to Roy Mohon, Muriel married Cyril Ashton formerly of Coxhoe, now Bishop of Doncaster. Muriel & Jean Roy's wife are my wife's half cousins and her Grandfather is on the right of the photo on page 242 of the Ward family. Hope this info helps. Bill.

Positive Jack and Annie Chisholm, Denis Chisholm (2nd right) 1st left one of the Mann family, centre back Billy Carr: I'm emailing you another copy of the street party Bernie, I hope it comes through bigger. Derek and I went to Coxhoe at the weekend to see exactly where it was taken, the table was on the road in front of the house where my Aunt and Uncle lived, Jack and Annie Chisholm, No 48 Green Crescent, they were the parents of Jack, Gillian, Jennifer and Jacqueline. Below: Commercial Road, just below the mineral line; showing everyday life, a scrap cart, the other possibly scissor grinding. Bikes were popular, a gentleman and woman riding one, another standing outside the 'Old Red Lion' Hotel; 'The Tyneside Inn' can also be seen.

An article appeared in the 'Coxhoe Chronicle', written by Mr. Joe Tweddle and which I am featuring in my book.
Kenny Ridley lived at 1, Tyneside Cottages, above, for many years and where he exhibited his garden furniture.
Kenny sadly died. (Kenneth Ridley/RIDLEY on March 25 (suddenly in hospital), of Coxhoe. Kenneth, aged 76 years. Ken Ridley [son of Robert Ridley & Harriet E. Bell] of 1, Tyneside Cottages, Coxhoe),

MEMORIES OF KEN RIDLEY

Ken was born in 1934 in No 1 Tyneside Cottages (Next to the Old Red Lion and a former pub, The Tyneside Arms) and was the youngest of 5. He had 2 sisters and 2 brothers. His father was a quarryman and, in the old tradition, his mother was a housewife.

Brother Bob was killed in an accident at the quarry in Doggy (West Cornforth) whilst brother George was a miner who lived until he was 86.

Ken went to school in Coxhoe both to the junior school and secondary. The headmaster was Mr. Potts and the subjects he enjoyed most were woodworking and gardening taken by Mr. Trewick and science taken by Mr. Soulsby.

On leaving school at the age of 15, Ken went to work for F W Dobson who had a quarry near the 3 Bridges at "Doggy". He went into the joinery shop and initially was making wooden wheelbarrows which were used to load trucks as all trucks were loaded by hand. He also learned some blacksmiths work which has stood him in good stead over the years.

At the age of 18, Ken went into the army for his national service. He was in the Royal Engineers and spent some time in Germany based at Hamelin (Pied Piper country). He was taught to drive and spent some time as duty driver on SDS duties ferrying around officers. He used to enjoy NAAFI nights on a Friday but wasn't so keen on sleeping rough when on exercises, living on NAAFI rations.

When he finished his national service, Ken went back to F W

Dobson's but they were eventually taken over by Tarmac and Ken was paid off. He spent 8 months on the dole before joining Raisby, still doing joinery work but also driving dump trucks and working with the drilling and blasting team. He enjoyed his time with Raisby and was there until he retired at the age of 65. As a younger man, Ken was keen on cycling and was a

member of the Coxhoe Cycling Club which met in the Old Red Lion, immediately next door to where he now lives. One of his brothers had a win on the pools and bought him a brand new bike which was his pride and joy. All the cyclists used to leave their bikes in an alleyway behind the pub which is now were Ken displays his garden ornaments. He has memories of local boxer Billy Bateson who used to train in the big room above the pub and Walter Salisbury who was a well known walker. Kens main interest throughout his life has been making things. He used to make layouts for model railways as well as rocking horses. He currently displays his wares on the plot of land where the Old Red Lion used to stand and part of Kens gable end is the window of what was the singing room of the pub. Ken tries to recycle materials for his models and is constantly on the lookout for cycle wheels and timber which he can put to use.

Hilda Scorer (right) Cornforth Lane School; about 1919.
Mother Hilda Scorer (later Morris) was born in 1912.

THE SCORER FAMILY

After his involvement fighting for his country Anthony Scorer was employed as a rolleyman (delivered produce by horse and cart) for Coxhoe Co-operative Store and he also took great pride in looking after the horses. He was the grandson of Anthony Scorer who was one of the founders of Cornforth & Coxhoe Co-operative Society Ltd., and was President for a few years. Unfortunately, after being promised £1 from 100 people to enable the Co-op to get started, only about one third honoured their promise. This may have contributed to certain financial difficulties later on. Like many other families the Scorers had tragedy in their lives through losing loved ones in the coal mines. Anthony and his wife Isabella lost two sons, John in 1859 aged 16 years, due to a fall of stone and in 1860 Thomas was run over by a tub of coals. He was only 13 years old. To take the initiative founding the Co-op during such hard times was a very brave thing for these men to do.

COXHOE GIRLS CLUB about 1959

L/R: B. Gilmore, M. Hutchinson,
C. Robson, S. Scott, J. Platts, A. Pattison, M. Lowe,
V. Lumley, D. Morris, E. Jackson, J. ....,
B. Hutchinson, M. Turner, D. Brownless, D. Wilkinson.

Anthony Scorer, right above, below left: Involved with COXHOE Co-operative with two of the wonderful horse and carts the store was known for. This is in the field behind St. Mary's Church. The man on the left holding the reigns is again A. Scorer. I would be interested to know the other person in the photograph is and who the other men in the photos are.

Above: Another Co-operative Store cart obviously advertising the good's available at the Multi–store. Below: The 'Kicking Cuddy', was called ' The Clarence Villa', once a private residence named after the Clarence Railway; later known as the Clarence Villa Hotel in the late 1800's was later renamed the 'Kicking Cuddy'. Cuddy races were run from the drive entrance of West Hetton Lodge to the Clarence Villa Hotel, it was also a coaching inn, both of which are linked to its current name.

ANTHONY SCORER at War

This photo was taken some time between December 1915 and June 1916. Anthony joined the Kings Own Lancaster Regiment and was sent to Salonika, Greece in June 1916. He and his fellow servicemen would arrive when heat (110 degrees f) and flies were unbearable. If marching north there was a problem with heat stroke. Water was very precious and if the soldiers were being shelled there was no food and the water supply was a long way off. Their main source of food was bully meat, which wasn't nice at all. The men were issued with steel helmets in September 1916 but were unable to wear them because of the heat. By November it was bitterly cold and the trenches were full of water. Anthony contracted malaria in 1917 and attacks lasted until at least 1921. He was lucky to survive as a large majority of soldiers died of this. He was also shot in the hand. On the 26th October 1917 he would probably be with his battalion when, after walking for 3 hours and only covering a mile due to the heavy rain and it being night time, the Kings Own Lancaster's attacked a Bulgarian garrison and took near 450 prisoners. In the 2nd Battle of Dorian in September 1918 there were a lot of casualties, with hand to hand fighting. The Armistice was on the 29th September 1918. The British Army in Salonika was to an extent forgotten, due to the events on the Western front, but never the less they were an important part of the

Anthony Scorer; 1915/16, Kings Own Royal Lancaster Regiment no 25781

Regiment no 25781

This photo was taken some time between December 1915 and June 1916. Anthony joined the Kings Own Lancaster Regiment and was sent to Salonika, <u>Greece in June 1916</u>

First World War. The Bishop of London commented, 'These men of the Eastern armies have had the dust & toil without the laurel of the victory'. Anthony Scorer enlisted in the British army on the same day as his step brother in law, Alfred Heron, on the 1st. December 1915, Alfred was a corporal in the 'Durham Light Infantry' & was sent to the Western Front. He lost an arm and was taken prisoner some time in May 1918. His brother John W. Heron was in the Royal Lancaster Regiment & was in France for the duration of the war. Their half cousin, William Crisp Scorer, was in the Lincolnshire Regiment and was in Flanders France he died in Cardiff Hospital on 5th November 1918. He was only 20 years old. The Scorer family, like many other families, certainly gave considerably for their country and living relatives should feel very proud of Anthony Scorer.

Cause of the Campaign: *From a report by Chris Morton:*
Bulgaria attacked Serbia in October 1915. This new threat led Serbia to appeal to the British and French governments for military assistance. At the same time Greece asked the Allies for help with their treaty obligations to Serbia. The British and French sent a small force which began landing at the Greek port of Salonika (Thessalonica) at the end of October. They advanced into Macedonia but were too late to help the Serbs who had to retreat through the Albania mountains. The Allies then withdrew back to Salonika and set up an entrenchment camp around the town known as the "Bird cage" and waited for the Bulgarians to attack. The Bulgarians did not advance on Salonika, but instead consolidated their gains in Macedonia. The British continued to build up their forces, and by early 1916 the force had increased from just the 10th (Irish) Division to the 10th, 22nd, 26th, 27th and 28th divisions. The Allies advanced up to the Serbian frontier and liberated Monastic. Trench warfare then began. The Allies attacked in the spring of 1917, but failed to break through. However, in September 1918 they attacked again and within two weeks had obtained Bulgaria's unconditionally surrender. The campaign in Macedonia was considered by many to be a "side-show". The Allied army was known back home as the "Gardeners of Salonika" due to the apparent lack of activity and people would comment *"If you want a holiday, go to Salonika"*. Despite the view of those at home, life in Macedonia was far from easy. The British Salonika Force not only had to cope with the extremes in temperature but also malaria. In 1916 it was possible to evacuate the most serious cases. However, with the introduction of unrestricted submarine warfare in April 1917 this was no longer possible. Consequently the cases of malaria soured as the infected men were compelled to stay in Macedonia. Hospital admissions in 1917 alone were 63,396 out of a strength of about 100,000 men. By early 1918 the British were again able to evacuate the worst cases and under the 'Y' scheme nearly 30,000 were evacuated. Many men suffered numerous relapses made worse by having to remain in Macedonia. Even when they were finally evacuated many would still suffer relapses for many years to come.

Above: A map of the area; *from a report by Chris Morton.*

Below: British troops taking their daily quinine issue of 5 grains on the Salonika front, July 1916.

The Amazing Long Row, built by Colliery owners to house their employees. Situated from the Basic works right to the end of the Co-operative store, my family lived at No. 25. Having site of all census forms nearly all of the families were employed, one way or another, to Collieries and Quarries. Below: The Mineral line 'Commercial Road', the photographer has captured every day life as it went on 'The Tyneside Inn', can be seen as can the 'Old Red Lion 'on the right.

Above: 'The Mill', about ½ mile from Coxhoe Hall and part of the estate; carried out all of the Hall's need for all farm foods especially corn for bread for the kitchens. There was a natural sand shore where the stream gently flowed towards Coxhoe Bridge & West Cornforth. As kids we picnicked here with a bottle of water and a jam sandwich, the scenery was breathtaking especially prior to the Hall being demolished and we spent hours here in School Holidays where we played football & cricket. My initials must be on nearly every tree. Below: The level crossing allowing access to the Basics for the mineral line to cross the road at the bottom of Coxhoe.

Park Hill Estate; built to ease the demand for Council housing in and around Coxhoe. There was also a demand for housing for workers at local Collieries and Quarries, all now modernised when, under a Thatcher Government, tenants were allowed to purchase their homes.

Beechfield Rise, Coxhoe came with the demand for better housing in the area, after Thatcher opened the housing market out by allowing people to purchase and improve their original Council housing for profit; this combined with low interest mortgages made people property millionaires.

The Laing Family of Coxhoe:

Private James Laing served his Country in the Great War, first of all in the 8th. Battalion DLI, where he received his initial training in 1914/15. By mid 1916 he was in the thick of the action in France; the 8th. Battalion was at that time part of the 50th. (Northumbrian Division) he saw action at the 'Battle of the Somme', 'The Battle of Ypres' & later, in 1917, the 'Battle of Arras'. James transferred into the 6th. Battalion 'Kings Own Yorkshire Light Infantry' which was part of 14th. Light Division; he was again right in the thick of it when serving on the 'Western Front' in 1917. This particular unit was disbanded in February 1918 but James Laing's war was not over yet and he again transferred to the 9th. Battalion Kings Own Yorkshire Light Infantry, being part of the 21st. Division. James Laing served with them on the Western Front in the final bitter actions in 1918; then he was demobilised in 1919. Mr. Laing it would seem was not going to leave the Battlefield until he had served every minute of his time even though at one time suffering from gas inhalation he had survived one of the bloodiest wars in history serving his complete time; thousands of British men never survived this horrible war which did not solve any problems and England was to go back to war with Germany 20 years later when our Country again suffered the loss of thousands of excellent British men. About 1919 James Laing returned home to Durham where it was his dream to farm in the area of Coxhoe and it was here that he met and married Lilly, nee Oliver, prior to the war. Later they took possession of the family 'Grange Farm', and this is where the couple started their family; James worked around the clock taking on any contract or work that was available until the farm was properly established. James was at the helm of the business during the hard recession period of 1926. With the coming of the second world war and as years passed when James and Lily sadly died the family traded on; for years the front shop was an Ice Cream shop owned by an Italian family 'Panicos' who sold wonderful ice cream. The Laing's took over the shop and 'Laings Sweets & Newspaper' business was born. The shop is brilliantly run by Margaret, Dickie's wife and it retains its *'Old World'*, charm with its high glass counter and courteous personal service.

The 1914-18 War
In the spring of 1916 the German army attacked in force in France. They were stopped in their tracks by allied forces 30 miles from

WESTERN FRONT *early 1916*

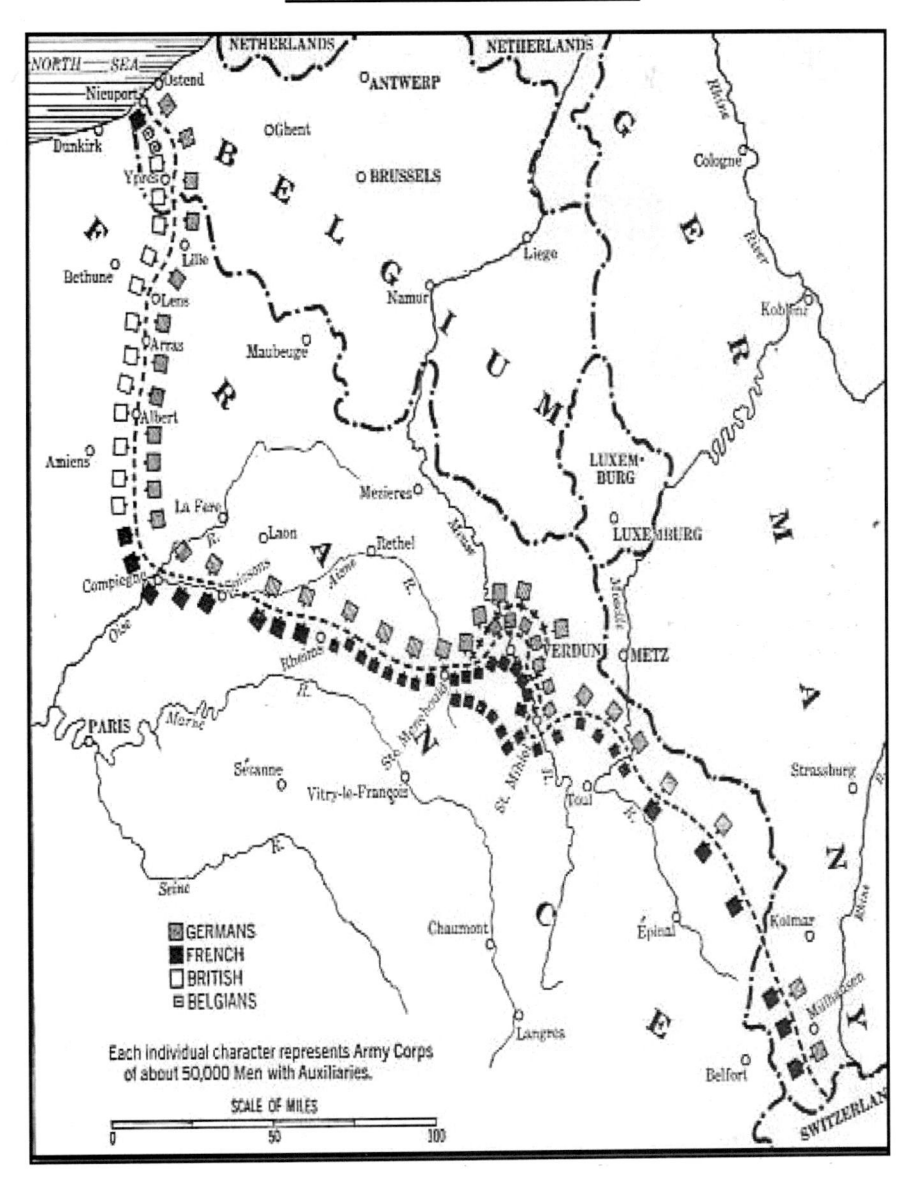

The Western Front. A series of trenches were evident running from the Belgian Coast to the Swiss mountains; neither Army was able to outflank the other. To try to bring pressure to bear on the Germans the Allies carried out a series of attacks in different areas of the front line at the Somme, (1916), Arras & Artois (1917), Ypres the same year (1917). Sadly there was tremendous loss of life in all three actions, not even taking into account smaller actions. In 1915 & 1916 a confident German army attacked the allied trenches at Ypres & Verdun. At sea Germany had built up a formidable fleet of submarines in the Atlantic and on the 7th May 1915 Walter Schwieger, the Captain of U20 submarine, gave the order to sink the beautiful four funnel Cunard liner 'Lusitania' which sank in twenty minutes with the loss of 1198 passengers which included 128 Americans; the Germans stated that the ship was carrying arms for the allies (later proved true). President Woodrow Wilson demanded Germany to disavow the sinking and make reparations. The Germans agreed to make reparations and not sink any further passenger ships but Schwieger defied his superiors and sank 'Hesperian', on 4th September, then a further five steamers in the course of five days, 'Druro', 'Rea', 'Dictator', 'Bordeaux' & 'Caroni' leaving America no choice but to declare war on Germany in April 1917. This could not have happened at a better time for the Allies because Russia was on the brink of collapse because of the war on the Eastern front and in December they signed an armistice.

This gave Germany the initiative when they moved all of their forces onto the Western front in an effort to quickly end hostilities before the American troops could arrive. The German army attacked in force on the 21st March 1918 and pushed the allies back when the action continued for month's, all of the time the allies were reinforcing and planning a counter offensive and this was the second battle of Marne in July of that year; the allies again planned a further attack in great force in August and this was known as the last 100 days of the war. The Germans retreated, a beaten army, they lost hundreds of men against now, a better and more organised, allied army.

The Laing Family History:
Great G. G. grandfather was John Laing born 1786 in Redmarshall near Stockton. He was a farmer married to Elizabeth Grey. It would seem they had 4 children of the marriage, one of whom is Great G. grandfather Thomas born in 1809 in Redmarshall.

In the 1841 census he was working as an engineman in Norton Junction and married to his 1st wife Rebecca. With the developing of the railways people were coming off the fields and working on the Railway. In the 1851 census Thomas was now in Coxhoe with his second wife Elizabeth Great G. grandmother and the children of his 1st marriage as well as their new baby also Thomas great grandfather. They were living in the Railway Tavern, Coxhoe, he was described as a farmer of 53 acres and Inn-keeper and it is interesting that Thomas Laing senior, when he died in 1858, was taken back to Redmarshall for burial which was quite an undertaking at that time, but perhaps it was because there was no church in Coxhoe then. Elizabeth met Thomas when she stopped off on her way to Durham to give evidence in a trial. They married in 1849 and she worked with him on various duties in the early delivery of mail, she was also step mother to 4 children. She must have had a tough life as she also had 4 children of her own. Thomas was born in 1850, he married Eleanor Bell daughter of a cobbler who originated from Cockermouth. John was born 1854, Isabella born 1856, Mary Jane Polly born 1857. Thomas and Eleanor remained in the Tavern (1891 census), but moved shortly after to the present family home of Grange Farm. They had 5 children; John Thomas born 1874, Frederick William born 1878, Isabella born 1880, James born 30-4-1887, married to Lily Oliver daughter of John Henry and Gertrude Regina Oliver. Beatrice was born 1890, James and Lily had 10 children; Gertrude who died as a baby when James was overseas, Eleanor, Sarah, Margaret (Peggy), Thomas and Gertrude Mary Maisie (*who died as a toddler after contracting measles*), John Henry (Jackie), Frederick Ernest (Dick).

The Laing connection with the Clarence Railway: (*Northern Echo story*)

Mrs. Elizabeth Laing died in her 86th year, at Coxhoe, she was the mother of Thomas Laing who was a well known Contractor at Coxhoe. In the early days the basic Clarence line ran from Coxhoe to Stockton, and was called the 'Clarence Railway Company'. Because of well known difficulties at the then Stockton drops, the Railway amalgamated with the 'Harbour and Hartlepool Railway', as early as 1852. Later they all merged, as part of the 'North Eastern Railway', in 1865. At that time the Chairman and controller of the then called 'W&H and H Railway', was no other than Mr. Jackson he surveyed & laid the Stockton & Hartlepool line.

Previously there was a stage coach that travelled from Durham to Coxhoe and then they caught the Train to Stockton and Thornaby, then later they embarked onto the 'Stockton & Darlington Line. At that time the coaches were very primitive and were simply seats around ordinary railway trucks, but everyone arrived safely at their destinations. The Wagons were drawn by a horse which covered the journey once a day; a Dandy or low Bogie on wheels were fastened behind the coaches. The horses were trained to ride on these Dandy carts on the return journey at inclines that usually ran all the way back to Sedgefield. When the driver/guard released the horse Mrs Laing distinctly remembers her first journey on the Railway, when she was very young she had to travel by coach to Durham City to identify some men arrested for stealing; shortly afterwards she returned to be a servant at the 'Blue Bell Inn', Coxhoe and where her future husband was Landlord. At that time the 'Blue Bell Inn' was the booking office for those who wished to travel by railroad or road, it was also the Parcel's Office and the Post Office for the district. Thomas Laing was Landlord of the 'Railway Hotel', in the years 1851, 1855 & 1856. The earlier named Blue Bell was an earlier beer house, about 1791, but is recorded as the Railway Tavern as early as 1841. It is listed in Red Row in the 1871 census, but seems to be called the Railway Hotel in later trade directories. The Railway Hotel was the booking office for the North East Railway and was also used as a coaching station. There was a 'Ball Alley' behind the hotel where championship games were played.

The Railway Hotel below

James and Lily Laing, the couple were married Carling Sunday, 9th of April 1916, later that year James would be in the thick of a thankless war in the trenches against a formidable foe, hell bent on killing as many good British men as possible. This photograph was taken during his initial training; James is very smart showing his button's and belt as regulation's, his boots bulled and wearing spats. Lilly is beautiful for the occasion with lovely styled dress, & hair. Soon James would be fighting for his very life in battle in the Great War in France.

Thomas & Eleanor Laing; 15/02/1850: the very beginnings of a powerful and amazing family the quality clothing and attention to their appearance and detail was first class.

Group outside of the Commercial Inn, 1st left, John Henry Oliver (Publican) 1906 aged 36. Woman second from right is Gertrude Laing, nee Smith, his wife. Small girl next to her is Lily who later married James Laing: John Henry Oliver seemed a giant of a man; I thought that it was the photograph but the man on the right was also tall but nowhere near the height of John Henry, who was the same height as men stood on boxes at the back, the height of Lily brings it in to perspective. Gentleman at the front had a straw boater, man on the right looked very prosperous and wore a watch and chain, no doubt silver or gold.

Gertrude Oliver, again the attention to detail on dress and appearance was brilliant.

The Oliver Family taken at the rear of the Commercial Pub, Coxhoe. L/R: Harry, John Henry, Lily, Gertrude/Regina, Arthur, Dick (Ernest). The dress and attire show they were a very prosperous family of the times.

Above, L/R: John Henry Oliver and Gertrude with Dick.
Right: Thomas Laing; year of his death 1933.
Below: A very early 'United Bus', Harry Oliver in cap 3rd, from left, at front, Jack Oliver with the stick. Obviously the start of a day out; the bus is parked outside of the 'Three Tuns'.

Below: William Smith, 1846-1919; Sarah Wiltshire, 1851-1906; parents of Gertrude Oliver.

Below: James Laing, with his brother Fred seated, in 1887, cutting corn somewhere near West Cornforth.

Thomas Laing, 1st on left, James Laing and his son 2nd on left, Frederick Laing holding the reins, John Laing was the Proprietor & brother of Fred and James, the 'Old Red Lion', one of at least three Inn's the Laings owned over this period. This photograph, in my opinion, is unique in that it shows the 'Tyneside Inn' next door to the 'Old Red Lion', at the time it traded, probably around 1900. There was obviously no problem with trading planning permission and public objections in those days as Inn's traded side by side. At the back of the Charabanc was a horse drawn buggy to service the main vehicle. There is an amazing one horse at the front as a lead horse with exceptionally long legs.

Lovely group photograph of the Laing and Oliver descendants; on my visit to Peggy I borrowed the picture from Peggy, breaking the glass in the process. L/R: Cyril, Bill, Ernest (dad), Edie, Mary, Peggy, Alice, Popsy, Vera, Olive, Mary, Jane nee Polkinghorn, father Ernest, Ruby, Elsie, Alan, Jean, Burt.

Left: Wonderful photograph of James Laing; it's as if it was posed with the dog's attention elsewhere. James returned from the War in France and began working the Land in and around Coxhoe.
Later below, around 1953.

In front of the Commercial Inn, Gertrude Oliver in Doorway;
Thomas Laing 1st on the left. Dated about 1902-3.

Group outside of the Commercial Inn, 1st right, John Henry Oliver (Publican), 1906, aged 36. Woman second from left is Gertrude Laing nee Smith, his wife, who was Licensee of the premises. One of the girls next to her is **Lily** who later married James Laing. Obviously a day trip in a horse drawn Charabanc. The driver was wearing goggles for the occasion and had a small terrier dog for company. The 'Commercial Inn' was next door to Lingfords grocery store, ideal for the Laing dynasty in Coxhoe. This must have been a special occasion, the men at the top of the picture are musicians, one playing a melodeon, the second a fiddle, the next seemed to be contemplating either to sing or to make a speech.

Mrs Lilly Laing nursing Eleanor, 1929.

Frederick Laing holding the horse; Tursdale Road, about 1900.

Below, L/R: Mrs. Robson, Mrs. Llewellyn, Lilly Laing, Mrs. T. Mayo.

Eleanor Sewell, nee Lamb, outside Chemist shop, 1930s.

James & Lilly Laing with, among others, Gertrude and Mary Lamb.

James Laing.
L/R: With son-in-law Ernest Chamberlain.
James with the horse and foal and with the baby.

Above: Thomas Laing as a young man, he was born 1851, the picture was taken in front of Talbot Row, Coxhoe.

Below: Thomas Laing, taken 1938.

Coxhoe from the West

I have seen this photograph so many times previously, no one ever did it justice on behalf of the photographer; with a general lack of pixels but guess who had the original picture 'The Laing family'.

It would seem the same photographer, the site of the Workingmen's Club

CORONATION YEAR. Outside Salvation Army Hall in West Parade:; Margaret Chamberlain, baby being held on right;, John Sewell, 3rd from left. 2nd Row: Further names for the group, the girl holding the little boy at the back is Joan Smith and the girl holding Margaret is Eileen Mulgrew. The little girl at the front is Annette Tennick with her brother Brian on the right (her left). Vincent Burke is hiding behind Annette. Out of interest, the Tennick's lived in the Gas houses round the corner from West Parade.

Above: Thomas Laing ,1938, James Laing in background.
Below: James and Lily Laing, 1950.

Lilly Laing feeding the hens; who says there are no free range eggs. In the background there are 4 milk churns, in early days the farm must have had a considerable herd of dairy cows.

Above, L/R: James and Lilly Laing; Margaret Chamberlain, 1952.
Below, L/R: Lilly Laing and daughter Eleanor Sewell, July 1952.
James Laing.

Below: Brilliant photograph of, L/R: Dickie Laing, Jackie Laing, with their nephew John Sewell, with the dogs, 1947.

L/R: Lilly Laing with Dora Collicot, nee Bell.

Below: James Laing with Pie Bald horse and foal; it would seem James Laing lived for his horses at this time in his life. All were in first class condition.

Right: Bob Sewell & Thomas Laing hoeing crops in the field.

Below: A happy young John Sewell with the sheep dogs, son of Eleanor nee Lamb.

Thomas Laing and Eric Symons, Donald Dee, James Laing, the horse in attendance, Ginger Prince. All busy laying pipes.

Top left: Jackie Laing, driving tractor.
Top right: Thomas, 1953.
Below: Thomas Laing.

Below: Thomas Laing and John Sewell in 1947. All of the family, it would seem, thought the world of young John Sewell, even the horse was paying special attention to him.

The above Water Colour apparently hung on the wall in the bar of the 'Railway Tavern', Coxhoe; the painting was entitled 'Pay Coxhoe Saturday'.

Jack Sewell, with his son John, with the pigs which seemed a special breed; it would appear that young John was very much at home with all animals as earlier photograph's indicate. These days school kids, after a visit to a farm, most of them contracted E/Coli; were kids in the fifties more immune to such things having a more nutritious diet?

The T.M.S. Bus Company

Trimdon Motor Services Limited (known as "The TMS") ran bus services through the areas of Coxhoe, Kelloe, Bowburn, West Cornforth and of course the Trimdons for many years. A comprehensive history of the company, written by Philip Kirk and Peter Cardno with the assistance of the last owner of TMS, Bob Lewis, was published in 2006. The following extracts and photographs are reproduced by permission of the authors.

The Original Directors

<u>Joseph Stanley Grundy</u>. Joe Grundy was born in September 1987 in Castle Eden and moved to Trimdon Grange when he was 18. His first vehicle was a Ford Model T, convertible between a bus and a lorry. On Tuesdays, Thursdays and Fridays it was used to deliver groceries from Boroughs of Wingate; on Saturdays the seats were refitted to take the local football team to matches; there were Church runs on Sundays and trips during the week to local markets and the cinema. This convertible was later traded in for a proper 14 seat bus, with a "Red Rose" emblem on the rear. In 1920, Joe married Ethel Woods of Fishburn.

<u>Roger Paul</u> was born in September 1887 at Ryhope, near Sunderland. By the time he married Ethel Logan in 1908 he was working at Trimdon Grange Colliery as a winding engineman and around 1920 he transferred to Fishburn Colliery. Roger felt the need to offer transport to people in the area and so he started a taxi business, and when he later returned to Trimdon Grange to work, he swapped the taxi for a Ford Model T.

<u>James William Seymour</u>. Jim Seymour originated in Cornsay Colliery near Tow Law and came to live in Trimdon Grange around 1913. He came into an inheritance in 1921 and with this he joined in a partnership with his great friend Roger Paul.

The Start of TMS

Joe Grundy had started a service between Fishburn and the Trimdons at about the same time as Paul & Seymour. Competition was tough with other companies such as Wilkinson's of Sedgefield and the soon-to-be mighty United both competing for customers. Therefore, Grundy, Paul and Seymour came together to coordinate their efforts rather than be in competition, and from about 1925 they were using the common fleet name "Trimdon Motor Services" or "TMS". The General Strike of 1926 was felt hard in the Durham coalfield and at its height the TMS decided to start its first regular

Left: Photograph taken early 1930 at Whitley Bay, on private hire.
L/R: Jimmy Seymour, Roger Paul and Joe Grundy.

Below: Joe Grundy with sister Louise, outside of their Leyland 'Lion' LT1, with locally built Edmond bodywork; the route board shows Hartlepool service.

Above: The TMS bus service was originally based at Trimdon Grange just opposite was Trimdon Grange Colliery.

Below: Trimdon Village, or Old Trimdon, there was also Trimdon Grange and Trimdon Colliery.

Above: Two Grundy REQ's lined up outside the garage in the 1920s, PT 8625, left, and UP 1246.

Below: Vulcan DR 1047 was in the Paul and Seymour fleet, route boards indicate Trimdon, very smart Dickie Wardle was the driver.

service from Trimdon Grange to the port town of West Hartlepool. A couple of years later this was extended west to Durham. In Durham, hackney carriages driving licences were issued to the three partners. In 1928 a new venture was started from Stockton via Castle Eden to Houghton-le-Spring and Sunderland, although this never really caught on and was cut back to run from the Trimdons to Houghton.

The days of cut-throat competition were coming to an end, with national regulations coming in 1931. These regulations were much tougher on bus operators who now had to have properly maintained buses and licensed conductors and drivers. For many, this was the end, but the TMS partners decided to gear up for the new regulations and so in November 1929 "Trimdon Motor Services Limited" was incorporated, with the three partners now becoming directors and assisted by Robert Thomas (the clerk at Trimdon Grange colliery) who acted as company secretary. The assets of the new company, including buses, petrol pumps, garages and cash-in-hand totalled £3,439/4/5.

The early 1930s were not a good time for anyone to be running a new business but TMS survived a threat of bankruptcy and thoughts that the directors might as well return to the mines. By 1934 things were looking up and TMS bought the County Motor Services business (a partnership of Dlongo Pearson of Spennymoor and Wallace Johnson of West Cornforth) with a route from Durham to Ferryhill via Coxhoe and West Cornforth.

From that time on, TMS flourished with private hire coaches being seen at every possible leisure destination at the north east including transport for the famous "Club Trips". The highlight of the year was of course Durham "Big Meeting" when it seemed like the whole county would descend on its cathedral city. Every possible TMS bus was pressed into service, and when each one filled up to the doors it would be sent straight to Durham, often the quick way via Signings Bank. Mrs Seymour would wait at her garden gate and the conductors would pour the takings into her pinnie before heading off again.

The war brought an end to much leisure traffic but it provided new opportunities to transport workers to the Royal Ordnance Factories such as that at Aycliffe, the biggest one of all. Troop movements were undertaken to as far as Aldershot and even Kent. Quite often, the authorities would commandeer buses (and sometimes drivers) and these would be stationed at locations for

Impressive photograph and line up of the Grundy Fleet, in 1928-29 all Reo, design; LR, 1146, UP 446, Pt 6646, PT8625

Above: Roger Paul with his Dennis Lancet which he was proud of UP 9684 on regular monthly trips to Blackpool; this photograph actually found in Roger's wallet after his death, 25 years since being taken.
Below: First Dennis Lancet PJ 5156.

months at a time. With the coming of peace, the demand for travel boomed as people who had been restricted in their habits wanted to enjoy the new freedom. TMS tried its best to keep up with the demand and it had to buy whatever new buses were available. Before the war the Dennis "Lancet" chassis was the favourite but in the late 1940s it bought A.E.C., Maudslay, Daimler and Bedford buses and coaches. By 1952, TMS had 30 vehicles which carried 3.7 million passengers. It was more than 25 years since the three directors had come together and with Jimmy Seymour now 70 and Roger Paul 65 it was decided to sell the business.

New Owners

William Henry Brunskill was born in Bishop Auckland in 1916, into a family of hauliers. Harry's first love, however, was flying, and the outbreak of war allowed him to join the RAF (even though he was in a reserved occupation) where he served with great distinction, including being awarded the Distinguished Flying Cross for his bravery. After the war, the government nationalised the road haulage industry and so in 1947, Harry bought the Favourite Direct bus company, based in Bishop Auckland with a service to Middlesbrough via Rushyford, Sedgefield and Stockton. This company had ten buses and was not generating enough money to buy TMS outright when it was offered for sale. Brunskill therefore put together a consortium which was able to buy TMS in April 1953 for £90,000.

John Richard Griffiths. Dick Griffiths was from Stockton, born in 1910. His trade was in butcher's shops before joining the Tank Corps during the war. After 1945 he developed Charlton's Car Sales of Norton, which was where he came into contact with Harry Brunskill who had a car sales outlet in Bishop Auckland.

After buying TMS, the new owners quickly expanded by buying up Alton Brothers of Trimdon Grange, which brought more new routes (Spennymoor – Ferryhill and West Hartlepool – Sedgefield). They also bought fifteen second-hand Daimler double deckers from London Transport to run these new routes.

At the end of 1953, however, Brunskill left the consortium to buy back the haulage company previously owned by his family; he also retained the previous Favourite Direct bus company, now retitled Transport Motor Services. This left Dick Griffiths in sole charge of TMS, and at first he invested a great deal, buying up J W Stewart of Horden (with local bus routes in Peterlee New Town) and Bluebird Coaches of Middlesbrough. He also bought ten new Sentinel buses and coaches. But after 1954 very little money was

Above: Harry Brunskill, top 6th from right, in his RAF days, with his Directorship came modern busses along with these Double Deckers, pictured in Stockton, one being a duplicate showing the increase in passengers:.

Above: Dick Griffith's on an official Blackpool trip.

Below: Very popular faces TMS Conductresses; Ellen Setterfield, Peggy Mitchell, Jenny Lee, Libby Woolhouse, Jane Athey and Annie Dawson.

Two of Griffith acquisitions with possibly no value at second hand.
Top: Sentinel STC 6, NNN998.
Bottom: A Dennis Falcon coach, VPA 261.

COXHOE & KELLOE *revisited* 2

Above: An impressive line up of Dennis Lancets outside the rebuilt garage, UP 9146, JH 2563, UP 9684, APT 657.

Below: The TMS Network in 1931, the Bus Company, however, just grew and grew.

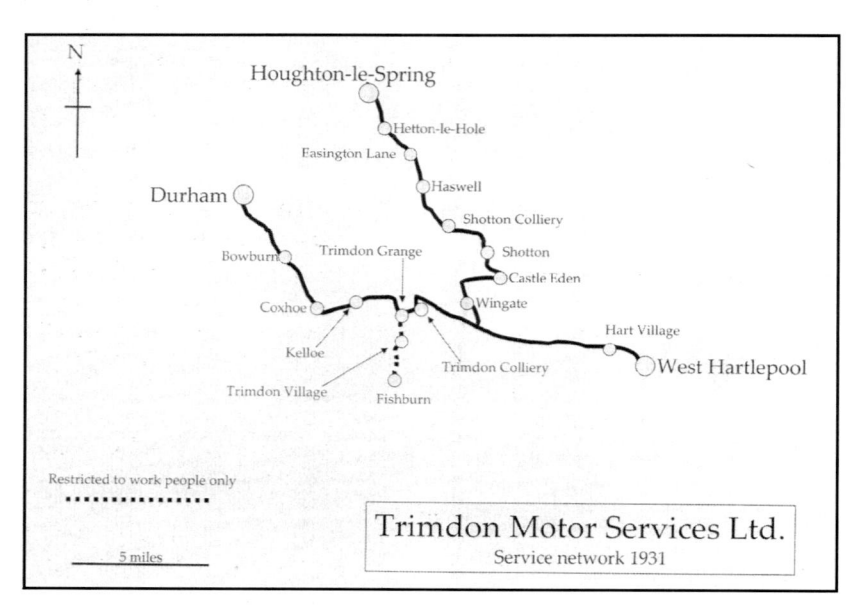

Trimdon Motor Services Ltd.
Service network 1931

spent at TMS and the fleet became run down. There was a national bus strike in 1957 which was inflamed at TMS and resulted in Griffiths locking out the staff. Griffiths decided he wanted to sell TMS and it was touted around local companies, including United, but without finding a buyer.

A New Dawn

<u>Robert Lewis</u>. Bob Lewis was born in Hepburn-on-Tyne in December 1924, and from the first he displayed his business acumen: as a young lad he collected driftwood from the Tyne, cut and bundled it and sold it door-to-door. He was apprenticed as a welder, and following service as a wireless operator during the war he did a variety of jobs including being a Butlin's Red Coat, where he met his future wife, Norma. Following an abortive emigration to Australia, Bob was back in England and married Norma in 1952.

On their honeymoon in Leeds they saw demonstrated a carpet cleaning machine, which they bought with their savings of £120 and so "Bestway Cleaners" was born. This was the first in a succession of business ventures which culminated in the late 1950s with the Lewis's having two old buses as mobile shops on the new housing estates on South Bank. Bob Lewis was approached by his accountant – who also served as accountant to Dick Griffiths – who told him that there was a bus company for sale "in the collieries". Lewis went to Trimdon Grange late one night and saw all the money being paid in by the conductresses and thought he could do something with the TMS business. He bought it in 1959 for £67,000, with £15,000 in cash and then £500 per month for nearly nine years.

Lewis later claimed that he knew nothing about buses but he knew a fair bit about business. The old buses of the Griffiths days were swept away and replaced by modern, lightweight Ford Thames Traders which were kept for only a few years before being replaced. Very quickly, the Lewis formula clicked and helped by Joe Marsden as Traffic Manager and Eddie Fowler as Chief Engineer the company was soon making a lot of money. Lewis was able to buy up companies as their original owners came up for retirement – Harry Brunskill's Transport Motor Services; Scurr's of Stillington and Favourite Service No. 2 of Bishop Auckland. Wilkinson's of Sedgefield and Gillett Brothers of Quarrington Hill slipped through his grasp and fell to United, but the expanded TMS, with bright modern buses giving a reliable and efficient service were a feature of the Durham coalfield. If the 1960s had been about expanding

Above: Sid Lowe, Eddie Fowler, Joe Marsdon, Alan Atkinson, Albert Rutter and Dave Smith.

Below left: Bob Lewis and Eddie Fowler in 1986.

Below right: Joe Marsdon with Bob Lewis and Eddie Fowler with the decorated new Volvo car which was Joe's leaving present.

TMS elsewhere and Bob and Norma Lewis bought Heaps Tours of Leeds, Norfolk Motor Services and Granville Tours of Great Yarmouth. The crowning glory, however, was the purchase of Jersey Motor Transport in 1970 and the Lewis's subsequently moved to the island to live.

1980s – The Final Expansion

The Conservative government of the 1980s privatised and deregulated many industries and the bus industry was not immune. Long distance coach travel was deregulated in 1980, which meant that no licences were required for routes longer than 30 miles. Lewis used this new freedom to launch "Zebra Holidays" based at Trimdon Grange which was an innovator of direct-sell continental holidays. With a fleet of 24 bright yellow and black striped coaches, Zebra was soon joined by the purchase of Blueline, a coach company with a non-stop service between the north-east and London. The base in the capital was soon closed down and operations moved to Trimdon Grange.

In 1986 local bus services were also deregulated and so things returned to the days of Grundy, Paul and Seymour with companies competing directly on the road. As ever, Lewis was ahead of the game and TMS amassed a fleet of 35 second-hand buses, which were used in Stockton-on-Tees in competition with Cleveland Transit. This soon escalated into Middlesbrough and then Newcastle and finally Sunderland, until TMS and its associated companies were one of the largest in the UK – with over 250 buses they moved to modern premises at Trimdon Grange. By this time, TMS was one of the most profitable bus companies in Britain.

Below: Leyland Tiger C75 UHN, repainted in United colours, taken outside of the TMS Company offices ready for United ownership which was inevitable.

Above left: Office girls. L/R: Sheila Cook, Libby Woolhouse, Emilyn Moyle.
Above right: Allan Seymour at Almouth during the war years, collecting eggs and milk.
Below: Receiving a cancer charity cheque. L/R: Les Mould, Bob Lewis, Bob Colley, (Official Charity), Eddie Fowler, Joe Marsdon, George Chalmers.

Durham Big Meeting day in the fifties, standing in front of a Lancet coach. L/R: Miriam Tootal, Jack Paul, Audrey Young, Molly Turnbull, George Whitelock, Ellen Setterfield, 'Jock', Betty Ross, Tommy Backley, Hazel Kilding, Violet Cook and Lol Murrayfield. Below: At Elwick Show. L/R: Jack Alderton, Bob Mawson, Jane Athey, Albert Rutter and Violet Cook.

Above: An impressive line up of Thames Trader busses outside of the Trimdon Grange garage.
Below: The Retirement of Joe Marsden, L/R, Alan Atkinson, Irene Lynch, Jack Cuthbert, Bob Lewis, Jack Alderton, Norma Lewis, Billy Grey, Joe Marsdon, Stan Allison, Violet Cook, Willis Coulson.

Willis's retirement. L/R above: Frankie Freeman (tyre fitter), Jim Coughlin (inspector), Willis Coulson, Mark Oswald (driver), Don Bell (fitter), Ray Ellar (driver), Ralph Calvert (driver), Eddie Fowler.

Above: The then new office block, there was also facilities for fitting and general maintaining the expanding fleet of busses.

Below: New garage facility Trimdon Grange, amongst others Bob Lewis, Eddie Fowler, Chris Lewis, Bob Lewis.

Modernisation of the Fleet. Top: One of a batch of seven Willowbrook bodied buses MUP 692-8J and the last with the 'flying shield' logo. Below: First of a batch Leopard coaches (OPT933) with many brilliant features. These were luxury travel buses, no one could any longer call the TMS (Trimdon Muck Shifters), just part of Bob Lewis's plans for 1970.

TMS in 1980 was looking for a big name bus to standardise their growing fleet of busses; this was achieved by the purchase of 'Tiger Busses'. Produced, designed and manufactured by Leyland.
Above: Three Tigers, C74-6UHN, all with the popular PSV chassis. With the purchase came stability & reliability.
Below: A further Tiger at Sedgefield with Duple Dominant body.

Zebra Holidays; By 1982 Bob Lewis recognised the coming trend and fashion for Continental Holidays. Hard working families, especially in the North East, were looking to the Continent for fair price holidays in the sunshine after the decline in British holidays and the expensive air flights. Bob recognised a gap in the market; his idea was for a budget holiday linked with good Hotels on the Continent. By 1982 three new Leyland 'Leopard' coaches appeared at TMS; these coaches were different from other Tigers that Leyland produced, in-that they were fitted with air suspension with turbo charged 11 litre engines capable of 245BHP. These busses were in response to the Volvo with its 658 chassis.

By 1984 Zebra Travel was increasingly popular. The Zebra Company was very well thought out and did not need travel agents; people dealt with the travel company directly. A new booking centre was opened at Trimdon Grange with 33 office and booking staff who dealt with people very courteously. There was a massive advertising campaign which had cost £50,000, over three years booklets including all of the information needed for continental travel were produced with brilliant photography of the busses and hotels. Zebra Travel offered daily departure's to Spain, Italy and Austria from 90 pick up points, one holiday for example in the Costa Brava would only cost £78.

The Zebra operation went from strength to strength in the following years. It was noted that Bob Lewis's son Chris was now taking an active part in the planning of the holidays. By February 1985 'Zebra Coaches', became a vehicle owning company in its own right with its own operating licence; it was doing so well that 30 busses had to be transferred from the TMS holding company.

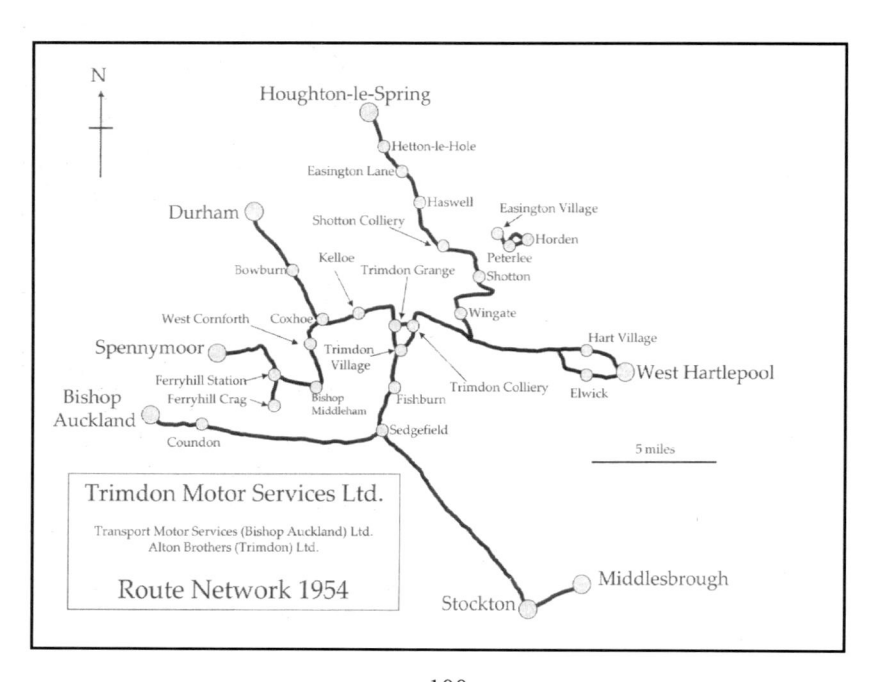

Trimdon Motor Services Ltd.
Transport Motor Services (Bishop Auckland) Ltd.
Alton Brothers (Trimdon) Ltd.

Route Network 1954

Above: One (A407 GPY) of eight Setra double deck coaches, bought at a cost of £1 million in 1984, which would revolutionise holiday travel.
Below: Chris Lewis accepting the keys for one of the Setra coaches.

Bob Lewis affectively put into place the Conservative change in the Transport Act when long distance coach tours including excursions and tours would be free from restrictions; all had to qualify with maintenance and finance standing when the operators licence was issued; it was also noted that a new bus grant was still in force until 1984.

THE END

In 1989 Bob Lewis was 65 and he reluctantly sold his bus interests on the UK mainland, and retired to his considerable interests in Jersey. The original part of TMS was sold to and then absorbed by United. TMS ran for the last time in September 1990, sixty years after its incorporation.

Early United Busses, the Company that later took over TMS, along with many other local once powerful bus companies.

Slater's Commercial Directory of Durham 1855 - COXHOE

COXHOE, THORNLEY, BLACK GATE, EAST HETTON
Quarrington Hill, Cassop & Ludworth

Post Office, Coxhoe, Thomas Laing, *Post Master* – Letters from London and all parts arrive every morning (from Ferry Hill) about eight, and are dispatched there to every afternoon about four.

Post Office, Thornley, Elizabeth Cossgrove, *Post Mistress* – Letters from London and all parts arrive every morning from (Ferry Hill) about half-past eight, and are dispatched there to every afternoon about half past three.

Academics and Schools

Boyes Elizabeth	Coxhoe Colliery School East Hetton – Andrew Fraser, master; Mary Bow, mistress
Craman Thomas	Cassop
Eelles William	Ludworth
Hay Thomas	Coxhoe
Huddart Mary	Cassop
Lawson Robert	Thornley
Lazonby John	Thornley
National School,	Thornley – John Dodd, master
Park William	Coxhoe
Sanderson Ann	Cassop
Scott Thomas	Coxhoe
Usher John	Thornley

Blacksmiths

Bulmer John	Garmondsway Moor

Cousen William — Black Gate
Liddell William — Thornley
Picken William — Black Gate
Williamson Thomas — Coxhoe

Boot & Shoe Makers
Bell John — Black Gate
Bell John — Coxhoe
Crofton William — Thornley
Dent Thomas — Quarrington Hill
Foster Robert — Thornley
Gibbon Henry — Thornley
Hood Richard — Thornley
Liddell John Thompson, Thornley
Oliver Elizabeth — Black Gate
Place Thomas — Black Gate
Robinson William — Thornley
Sayer Charles — Cassop
Swinton Thomas — Black Gate
Temple James — Cassop

Brewers
Allison Cuthbert — E Hetton
Richardson John — Cassop
Richardson Matthew — Coxhoe Lane End
Scott Thomas — Coxhoe Station

Brick & Tile makers
Birkett Thomas — Coxhoe
Carnaby Ralph — Black Gate

Butchers
Carr George — Black Gate
Clark Edwards — Thornley

Clark James	Coxhoe
Clark John James	Thornley
Lockey James	Black Gate
Pickering John	Black Gate
Robinson Joseph	Cassop
Scott George	Thornley
Siddle Robert	Cassop
Simpson William	Thornley
Stonehouse John	Coxhoe
Strofhuir William	Coxhoe
Swinburn Robert	Thornley
Wanless Bateman	Thornley
Watson George	Quarrington Hill
Weals John	East Hetton
Wight Charles	Ludworth
Wright Thomas	Thornley

Colliery Owners

Cassop Colliery Company, Cassop - Ralph Henry Philipwinsop, manager; William Hall, viewer.

Crow Trees Colliery Company - Heugh Hall, Bowburn, & West Hetton - John Robson head viewer; Richard S Johnson, resident agent.

East Hetton Colliery Company, East Hetton - Percival Forster, manager; Thomas E. Forster, viewer; Anthony Brydon, under viewer.

Ludworth Colliery Company, Ludworth - Thomas Wood, manager; Joseph Smith, resident viewer.

South Kelloe & Coxhoe Colliery Company - John Robson, head viewer; Richard S. Johnson, under viewer.

Thornley Colliery Company, Thornley - Thomas Wood, manager; Joseph Smith, resident viewer.

Grocers, Drapers & Shopkeepers

Anderson Thomas	Coxhoe
Arrowsmith John	Thornley
Atley John	Coxhoe
Beecroft George	Thornley
Cock William	Blackgate
Crofton William	Thornley
Cutter John	Ludworth
Dines Robert	East Hetton
Elliot John	Thornley
Embleton John	East Hetton
Greenwell Richard	Thornley
Hall George	Cassop
Harrison William	East Hetton
Jackson John	Thornley
Jackson Robert	Thornley
Johnson Mary	Thornley
Joplin Thomas	Blackgate
Liddell John Thompson	Thornley
Liddell Joseph	Coxhoe
Liddell William	Thornley
Martin Matthew	Thornley
Matthew William	Cassop
Newton James	Coxhoe
Norman William	Thornley
Pearson & Gomersail	East Hetton

Joiners & Cabinet Makers

Allison John	Quarrington Hill
Arrowsmith William	Thornley
Best John & Cartwright	Black Gate
Ramsay Thomas Smith	Thornley

Surgeons
Cairns John	Black Gate
Scott William	Thornley

Tailors
Anderson James	Coxhoe
Carr Aaron	Black Gate
Carr William	Coxhoe
Donaly Edward	Cassop
Graham Joseph	Thornley
Heightley Robert	Quarrington Hill
Herbert Ralph	Ludworth
Newby John	Thornley
Oliver John	Thornley
Lonsdale Robert	Thornley
Sutton Robert	Cassop
Thompson Thomas	Quarrington
Turner George	Coxhoe
Urwin John	E Hetton

Taverns & Public Houses
Black Boy	Robert Hindmarsh	Quarrington Hill
Black Bull	John Bainbridge	Thornley
Black Bull	Martha Sotheran	Cassop
Black Horse	Richard Brown	Thornley
Black Horse	Thomas Cummings	Black Gate
Braddyll's Arms	Eleanor Allison	E Hetton
Bridge Inn	William Carr	Coxhoe
Bridge Inn	Thomas Scott	Coxhoe
Cassop Inn	Edward Robson	Cassop
Clarence	William Strofhair	Coxhoe
Colliery Inn	Richard Smithson	Thornley
Commercial	Thomas Fidler	Coxhoe
Cross Keys	James Taylor	Quarrington
Crow Trees Colliery Inn	Thomas Thompson	Quarrington

Davy Lamp	Matthew Richardson	Coxhoe Laneend
Dun Cow	Joseph Ward	Thornley
Dun Cow	William Wilson	Quarrington
Engine	Stephen Bone	Thornley
Forresters Arms	Thomas Harrison	Cassop
Fox & Hounds	Thomas Bell	Garmondsway Moor
Prospect House	George William	Greenwell
Good Intent	Thomas Heron	Quarrington
Grapes	Thomas Blenkinsop	Cassop
Grapes	John Richardson	Jun Coxhoe
Grey Horse	Thomas Williamson	Coxhoe
Greyhound	Margaret Crow	East Hetton
Greyhound	Christopher Swinbank	Black Gate
Half Moon	Matthew Smith	Quarrington
Heugh Hall	Mar Foster	Heugh Hall
King's Head	Wm Binks	Thornley
Letters	William Cock	Black Gate
Letters	Nicholas Cousen	Black Gate
Letters	Matthew Ranson	Cassop
Letters	John Smith	Old Thornley
Letters	John Tate	Thornley
Ludworth Inn	John Jameson	Ludworth
Mason' Arms	William Tweddle	E Hetton
Newcastle Arms	Roger Bell	E Hetton
New Inn	William Garthwaite	Oak Tree
	Thomas Robson	Quarrington
Prince Albert	Ralph Raffel	Cassop
Queens Head	John Arrowsmith	Thornley
Queens Head	William Lonsdale	Ludworth
Railway Tavern	John Brydon	E Hetton
Railway Tavern	William Carr	Cassop
Railway Tavern	Thomas Laing	Coxhoe
Red Lion	Mark Hogg	E Hetton

Red Lion	Elizabeth Oliver	Black Gate
Robin Hood	George Scott	Thornley
Seven Stars	John Wanless	BlackGate
Spearsman's Arms	John Bowman	Thornley
Standish Arms	Jonathan Stephenson	Ludworth
Three Horse Shoes	William Liddell	Thornley
Three Tuns	Stephen Best	Black Gate
Three Tuns	Thomas Featherstone	Coxhoe
Turks Head	John Liddel	E Hetton
Tyneside	Mary Lynn	Coxhoe
Victoria	Thomas Jameson	E Hetton
Victoria	John Richardson	Cassop
West HettonTavern	John Currie	Coxhoe
Wynyard Arms	Jonathan Spelding	Kelloe

Retailers of Beer

Fletcher John	Thornley
Gates Thomas	Coxhoe
Gedson John	Thornley
Patton Thomas	Thornley
Robson William	Thornley

Miscellaneous

Bayley James	newsagent	Thornley
Batey James	greengrocer	Cassop
Milburn Thomas	marine store dealer	Thornley
Pigford Robert	greengrocer	Thornley
Rowe William	tobacco pipe maker	BlackGate
Saver James	marine store dealer	Thornley
Temple James	tea dealer	Cassop
Turnbull Martin	iron founder	Coxhoe
Welsh John	watch maker	Coxhoe

Railway

There is a *Station* at Black Gate, on the York, Newcastle and Berwick Line – Thomas Scott, *station master*, also at Coxhoe, on the West Hartlepool Harbour & c.Lines – Jas Porter, *station master*.

Bernard McCormick worked at Bowburn Colliery after leaving Cornforth Lane School. After five years he left the pits and completed his National Service with the 13/18 Royal Hussars, in Malaya during the Emergency where he saw active service. After being demobbed he married his wife Eileen, then worked twenty years in Engineering. Later he ran a successful designer clothing business. Bernie, now retired, writes extensively on Family and Local History. He has written four books on Northern and Scottish characters in the Northern and Scottish Folk series, and has researched, written and edited his family history, which includes four families. Bernard has also written books on North East Mining, including 'Troubled Collieries', which was a great success, especially in the North East; and which he is reprinting again and includes four more Collieries and an extra fifty pages; 'Northern Mining Roots' was published in 2006 and is also proving popular. Bernard is researching the Coulson's & Robson's on his mother's side, Jane Fletcher Coulson, who were all Colliery owners and shaft sinkers.

Bernie has written and published a pictorial group of books on Coxhoe and District, where he was born. In 2003 Bernard wrote 'Northern Folk 1 & 2 for Business Education Publishers Limited', *(Leighton),* as one volume of 24 stories of Northern Characters, the people who made the area what it is today. It even includes a greatly loved poetess, Elizabeth Browning. This book can be bought from the Leighton website on www.bepl.com or www.bermac.co.uk.

In 2008 'The Peases & the S&D Railway', was published which traces the early beginnings of the S&D Railway at Darlington and the people involved in establishing this brilliant time in North East History and is doing well. There are many orders for the current 'Coxhoe & Kelloe *revisited'* which also includes a reprint of 'Kelloe, Bowburn & Cornforth' All of the books can now be supplied as an E/Book on C/D Rom. There is a good variety of E/Books including, Irish Legends, the Northern & Scottish Folk series and Troubled Collieries and Northern Mining Roots, on one E/Book. In 2011 'Commanders of the British Isles', was produced, covering Clive of India, General Wolfe, Lord Nelson, Duke of Wellington, Fitzroy Somerset (Raglan) and T.E. Lawrence. **SCOTLAND** William Wallace, Robert the Bruce, Mary Queen of Scots, Charles Edward Stewart and Admiral Napier. £6 of the proceeds will be donated to the Commanding Officers Appeal for the dead and injured of Afghanistan at http://bermac.co.uk/e-book-commanders.html. This current book 'Coxhoe & Kelloe *revisited'* will be published about October 2011.